POCKET FILM PHILOSOPHY

3 ESSAYS

ISBN 9798902431398

Printed in the United States of America

$9.99

CONTENTS

CHAPTER ONE

Cinemagraphic Truth: Vertov, Montage, and the Deconstructive Logic of the Postal Principle

Introduction: Cinema as Communication and the Persistence of Realism

Like a postcard circulating through global postal networks, a film is a material message composed of text and images whose meaning must traverse a technological medium before reaching spectators. This seemingly simple analogy opens onto a complex history: cinema, from its inception, has evolved through both technological advances and narrative experiments designed to refine the forms of address available to it. Yet, as Peter Brunette and David Wills insist in Screen/Play, film theory has rarely considered cinema according to the same communicational logics that structure telecommunications and other media systems. Instead, most major critical paradigms reproduce a model of address grounded in identity:

"Auteurism relies on authorial intention… textual analyses assume a structured core of sense… spectator studies still describe the subject in terms of positionality" (185).

Brunette and Wills thus argue for a deconstructive attentiveness to cinema's postal features—its logic of sending, transmission, and failed arrival. Such an approach resonates with Derrida's discussions of the letter that never quite reaches its destination, and it is particularly illuminating when applied to a filmmaker like Dziga Vertov, whose theoretical writings and films hinge on questions of truth, perception, and mechanical inscription.

This essay situates Vertov's *The Man with the Movie Camera* within this larger problematic. Rather than reading Vertov solely through Soviet montage theory or Marxist constructivism, the analysis deepens the tensions already present in Vertov's own claims about kino-truth. The goal is to show how the film's self-reflexive strategies expose the contradictions inherent in any technological medium that claims unmediated access to reality.

Vertov's Kino-Truth: Mechanical Perception and the Ideal of Photographic Authenticity

Vertov's concept of kinopravda, often translated as "film truth," is grounded in a belief that the camera surpasses human perception. For Vertov, the camera is not merely a tool; it is an extension of the filmmaker's sensory and cognitive apparatus. It becomes, in effect, an all-seeing "I," capable of penetrating the fabric of reality in ways unavailable to the human eye.

This belief leads Vertov to describe the camera as producing an autonomous "cine-thing," an organic mechanism capable of expressing "life as it is." The camera's ability to record "life unawares" ostensibly frees cinema from the distortions of subjective perception. Such an ideal is consistent with

Nietzsche's notion of the "optical habit of seeking" truth (Will to Power 185), an impulse that equates seeing with knowing.

The kino-eye, then, becomes a means of producing a new visual structure—one rooted in ontological authenticity. Vertov imagines each film frame as a homogeneous whole, transparent to reality, unmediated by aesthetic codes. This position aligns closely with Roland Barthes's reading of the photographic image as a "message without a code" (Image-Music-Text17). For Barthes, the still photograph collapses the distance between signifier and signified; it becomes almost indistinguishable from the reality it records.

Vertov inherits and extends this logic to moving images, claiming that cinematic realism results from the camera's mechanical capacity for truth. The film frame, functioning as a perfect analog of reality, is treated as a direct imprint of the world. Such a view implies that cinema's authority stands above and beyond human interpretation.

The apex of Vertov's vision would have to wait for the invention of the Steadicam by Garett Brown in 1975. The Steadicam camera person is modern-day centaur, a new mechanical organism in which they and the camera morphed together into a single cinematic body. As Ferrara writes, "Wearing the Steadicam, the operator becomes something 'more', a new entity, united and separate; the Steadicam comes to resemble the mind's creativity, the fusion of what you see with your eyes and a viewfinder and what you imagine will be its best technical realization." (Ferrara 2001: 63)

The Steadicam operator is the ultimate imbrication of the human and technology, a hybrid technics of muscle and mechanics unique to the cinema. Below is how Eric Hynes sums this up (italics are mine):

> Steadicam shots are uncanny. They mimic how we move and see, and furthermore they seem to anticipate how we expect to be able to move and see, but can't…They do come from a body: a person is carrying the machine that's making these images, at human height, usually at human speed, moving and turning and observing…This is akin to how our bodies and eyes operate, except the technique doesn't settle for approximating how we move through the world; it makes improvements, surpassing our capabilities with a precognitive fluidity of movement…Steadicam shots are like tails to our tailbone, things beyond us that seem of us. They're both alien and familiar. (Hynes 2016: 29)

The Steadicam fulfils Vertov's dream of film-truth as a bio-mechanical process he first articulated 50 years prior.

Montage as Supplement: The Paradox of Constructing Truth

Yet Vertov's own practice complicates this claim. While kino-truth is grounded in photographic realism, Vertov insists that the true essence of cinema lies in movement, not stasis. The frame is never isolated; it is always part of a chain whose meaning emerges from the relations between shots. Montage therefore becomes indispensable.

This dependence introduces a fundamental paradox: if the frame contains truth, why must it be supplemented by montage? Vertov himself admits that "it is not enough to film bits of truth," for they must be organized into a "truth of the whole" (Michelson 18, 120).

Here, Derrida's logic of the supplement becomes illuminating. Montage both completes and disrupts kino-truth. It supports the frame while revealing that the frame lacks the fullness of truth it was presumed to contain. In this way:

- kino-truth is always already incomplete,
- montage becomes its necessary supplement,
- and the "truth" of reality is constructed rather than revealed.

Meaning thus emerges in the intervals—the gaps between frames. These intervals, invisible yet essential, enact a form of spacing that aligns cinema with Derridean writing. The splice becomes the site where truth is both produced and deferred.

Montage displaces the camera's claim to pure presence. Kino-truth, rather than a window onto the real, becomes a kinetic system structured by difference.

From Cinematography to Cinemagraphy: Writing, Trace, and the Postal Principle

Vertov formalizes his reliance on intervals in his Theory of Intervals, which posits that cinematic meaning arises from the movement between shots. This claim positions cinema not as a transparent photographic medium but as an apparatus of writing. The splice becomes analogous to Derrida's trace: an absent mark that structures presence. Thus:

- the frame resembles a grapheme,
- the sequence of frames functions like syntax,
- and the interval serves as the spacing that makes meaning possible.

The "kino-eye = kino-seeing + kino-writing + kino-organization" formula reveals Vertov's inadvertent acknowledgment of this logic (Michelson 87). Montage is not merely a technique; it is the writing of cinema. Vertov thus reinscribes cinema into the domain of textuality, despite his claims to photographic transparency.

This reorientation aligns Vertov's work with Derrida's postal principle, where meaning circulates through delays, reroutings, and failed arrivals. The cinematic message—like a letter—never reaches a destination without deviation. Kino-truth, paradoxically, becomes a form of adestination.

Constructivist Realism: Baring the Device and the Visibility of Mediation

Where classical narrative cinema seeks to conceal its operations, Vertov foregrounds them. Through the constructivist principle of baring the device, The *Man with the Movie Camera* exposes its techniques:

- editing tables,
- freeze frames,

- reverse motion,
- split screens,
- spatio-temporal manipulation.

The Man with the Movie Camera (1927) stages the dialectic of kino-eye and kino-truth not as a transparent epistemology but as a problem of cinematic mediation. The film's double movement—documenting everyday life while foregrounding the cameraman as a worker—renders perception inseparable from its technological conditions. By repeatedly revealing the camera and the labor of montage, *The Man with the Movie Camera* enacts a constructivist logic of self-exposure, "baring its own devices" to stage truth as a function of cinematic operations rather than mimetic access to reality. The camera figures as an "outside" that is irreducibly "inside," an apparatus that claims objectivity while marking the site of its own intervention.

What is at stake, however, is not simply cinematic self-reflexivity. The film turns on a circular process that simultaneously pursues "life unawares" and dismantles the illusion of unmediated vision that such a pursuit presupposes. This tension is not resolved but inscribed within the film's intervals—its cuts, splices, and gaps—where the discrepancy between Vertov's theoretical claims and cinematic practice becomes legible. Once again, read through Jacques Derrida's critique of representation, these intervals produce a series of "postal effects," in which truth is neither delivered intact nor simply revealed, but deferred, displaced, and structurally mediated.

From this perspective, Vertov's cinematography does not disclose the truth of representation; it exposes representation as undecidable between truth and perception. Kino-truth, understood as kino-perception, is constituted through difference, spacing, and technological inscription, aligning it less with visual transparency than with a logic of writing—an alignment clarified by Derrida's logic of the supplement which we discussed earlier. At the same time, the camera's appearance within the film operates as a technological signature, a self-indexing mark that insists on the fact of seeing. This signature displaces kino-truth from the image's center toward its margins, situating truth not in what is shown but in the cinematic conditions that frame, interrupt, and defer its appearance.

The film reveals the mechanics of representation, thereby educating viewers about cinema's grammar. This pedagogical aim reflects Vertov's Marxist commitment to raising visual consciousness.

Yet in baring the device, Vertov exposes the constructed nature of cinematic truth. The very techniques meant to reveal reality instead highlight its mediation. The kino-eye becomes not a transparent window but an apparatus that structures visibility. Its insistence on mechanical truth unravels into a demonstration of cinema's artifice.

The Camera as Signature: Authorial Presence and the Inside/Outside Problem

The camera's recurring appearance within the frame—most vividly in the superimposition of the camera lens over a human eye—functions as a signature of authorial presence. This signature is intended to authenticate the film's truth claims, marking the camera as both witness and guarantor.

However, Derrida's account of the signature complicates this function. A signature, once inserted into a text, loses its external authority and becomes part of the text's internal play of meaning: "By inserting it into the body of the text, you monumentalize it… erect it into a stony object" (Signsponge 56). The camera-signature destabilizes kino-truth. Rather than confirming presence, it reveals mediation. The splice—an absence rather than an image—thus becomes the decisive locus of truth. While the photographic image promises the "impression of the thing itself," montage exposes this immediacy as an effect produced through absence. Cinematography becomes cinemagraphic: a practice of inscription rather than revelation. The camera turns out not to be an eye but a pen.

It disrupts the distinction between inside and outside, objective observer and subjective participant. The signature becomes a common name, dispersed throughout the film, undermining the coherence of authorial intention.

The camera's self-inscription thus enacts a deconstructive reversal: what was meant to guarantee truth instead becomes the sign of its impossibility.

Conclusion: Kino-Truth as Adestined, Cinemagraphic Truth

Vertov sought to ground cinematic truth in the documentary immediacy of photographic realism. Yet his reliance on montage, intervals, and self-reflexive signatures reveals that kino-truth is always mediated, deferred, and constructed. The film's meaning arises not from the presence of the real but from the spacing and difference between frames. In this sense:

- kino-eye discloses not unmediated truth but the conditions of its impossibility,

- montage produces truth rather than revealing it,

- and the camera's signature signs not transparency but illusion.

Cinematic truth is thus cinemagraphic: a form of writing structured by différance, governed by the postal principle, and destined never to arrive fully at its intended meaning. Vertov's own techniques—meant to fuse perception and truth—ultimately expose the fissures that render kino-truth an adestined message, wandering without arrival. The combination of kino-truth and kino-eye means truth in Vertov's theory and practice is undecidable.

CHAPTER TWO

The Eternal Return: Time and Desire in *Nostalghia*

Introduction: Cinema, Nostalgia, and the Crisis of Time

In *Sculpting in Time*, Andrey Tarkovsky characterizes cinema as a fundamentally nostalgic art. Film, he argues, is uniquely capable of returning to the same event repeatedly, allowing the past to reappear in the present of projection. Yet his film *Nostalghia* does not merely thematize nostalgia as longing for what has been lost. Instead, it transforms nostalgia into a crisis of temporality itself. The film presents a world in which the past does not recede into memory, the present fails to stabilize experience, and the future appears only as catastrophe or sacrifice. Nostalgia, here, is not a sentiment but a condition of existence.

Modernist cinema is frequently described as a cinema of crisis: crisis of narration, of subjectivity, of belief in linear history. Yet what distinguishes certain late modernist filmmakers is not simply the rejection of classical storytelling, but a sustained interrogation of time itself as an ethical and existential problem. Andrey Tarkovsky occupies a singular position within this tradition. His films do not merely abandon chronology; they expose the lived consequences of inhabiting a world in which time no longer guarantees meaning, continuity, or redemption.

Nostalghia (1983) emerges at a decisive historical and personal moment in Tarkovsky's career: his first film made outside the Soviet Union and the beginning of his permanent exile. While often read as an autobiographical meditation on homesickness, *Nostalghia* articulates a far more radical diagnosis. *Nostalghia* is not presented as longing for a lost homeland, but as a condition in which the present fails to sustain existence. The past does not recede into memory; it persists as an unresolved demand. The future offers no horizon of progress, only catastrophe or sacrifice.

Nostalghia occupies a pivotal position within Tarkovsky's broader exploration of time, memory, and spiritual responsibility. While earlier films such as Ivan's Childhood and Mirror already experiment with fractured temporality and subjective memory, they retain a residual confidence in memory's capacity to bind the self together. *Mirror* treats recollection as painful yet sustaining, a means of assembling identity from dispersed fragments. By contrast, *Nostalghia* marks a decisive shift. Memory no longer heals; it weighs. The past does not offer coherence but obligation. This shift anticipates the radical austerity of The Sacrifice, where time becomes inseparable from ethical decision and irrevocable loss. Seen in this light, *Nostalghia* functions as a threshold film: poised between autobiographical remembrance and eschatological renunciation.

The figure of the task—the candle-crossing—links *Nostalghia* to *Stalker*, where characters undertake a journey, whose meaning lies not in arrival but in perseverance. Yet unlike Stalker, *Nostalghia* removes the possibility of collective redemption. The task must be completed alone, without recognition, without assurance that it matters. This isolation reflects Tarkovsky's growing conviction that spiritual responsibility cannot be delegated to institutions, narratives, or historical progress.

Within Tarkovsky's oeuvre, then, *Nostalghia* represents the moment when time ceases to be remembered and must instead be endured. This chapter argues that *Nostalghia* constructs nostalgia as a cinematic form of time rather than a psychological state. Drawing on Gilles Deleuze's theory of the time-image—particularly the crystal-image and chronosigns—I show how Tarkovsky renders time directly, as fracture rather than flow. The film's formal strategies—mirrors, doubles, water, ruins, ritualized action—produce images in which the distinction between past and present, dream and reality, actual and virtual becomes indiscernible. These images do not ask to be interpreted; they demand endurance, ones in which temporal distinctions collapse and desire is displaced from erotic fulfillment into spiritual obligation. I place Deleuze's film theory in dialogue with Jacques Derrida's figure of "cinders" and Friedrich Nietzsche's doctrine of eternal recurrence, contending that Tarkovsky renders time "out of joint" not as a philosophical abstraction but as a lived, spectatorial experience. The film does not represent time; it makes the fracture of time perceptible.

I also contend that *Nostalghia* stages a logic of return without recovery. The past remains not as origin but as residue; repetition intensifies experience without restoring wholeness. In doing so, Tarkovsky transforms cinema into an ethical encounter with time itself—one that implicates not only the protagonist but the spectator, who must inhabit the same temporal uncertainty the film refuses to resolve.

Exile and Narrative Minimalism

The narrative of *Nostalghia* is deceptively sparse. Andrei Gorchakov, a Russian poet, travels through Italy researching the eighteenth-century composer Sosnovsky, another Russian exile. Accompanied by his translator Eugenia, Andrei remains emotionally distant, repeatedly rejecting her advances. His refusal is not prudishness or indifference but incapacity: he cannot inhabit the present without betraying the past to which he remains bound.

The encounter with Domenico intensifies this condition. Domenico's belief that humanity can be saved through a ritual act—carrying a lit candle across St. Catherine's Pool—introduces a task that is both absurd and absolute. It demands patience, faith, and endurance rather than interpretation. Domenico's eventual self-immolation transforms this private conviction into public spectacle, exposing the gulf between spiritual urgency and collective indifference.

Tarkovsky deliberately strips the narrative of causal motivation. Characters do not develop; they persist. Events do not explain one another; they echo. This minimalism is not aesthetic restraint but temporal strategy. By refusing narrative resolution, Tarkovsky prevents the past from being absorbed into explanation and the future from functioning as promise.

Tarkovsky's Temporal Problem

Tarkovsky repeatedly insisted that cinema's task was not to tell stories but to "sculpt time." Yet cinema's technical condition poses a paradox: it must present time sequentially even when attempting to evoke simultaneity, memory, or interior duration. Tarkovsky acknowledges this limitation but refuses to resolve it through narrative convention. Instead, *Nostalghia* foregrounds the tension itself.

The film's images do not point backward or forward in time; they hover. Memory is not retrieved but endured. Dreams are not marked as dreams; they intrude into waking life. Tarkovsky's cinema thus aligns less with psychology than with phenomenology: what matters is not what happened, but how time is experienced when it no longer coheres.

Deleuze and the Time-Image

Gilles Deleuze's theory of postwar cinema provides the most precise account of this experience. Deleuze distinguishes the classical movement-image—where time is subordinated to action and narrative—from the time-image, in which time appears directly. In the time-image, the present no longer organizes experience; it becomes one element among others in a fractured temporal field. Tarkovsky is central to Deleuze's account because his films consistently suspend action in favor of duration. In *Nostalghia*, movement rarely advances narrative; it reveals hesitation, repetition, and exhaustion. Time does not pass; it weighs.

The Crystal-Image and Indiscernibility

The crystal-image is Deleuze's name for images in which the actual and the virtual—present and past—become indiscernible. This indiscernibility does not erase difference; it renders difference undecidable. Tarkovsky constructs such images through mirrors, doubles, and minimal perceptual shifts. Andrei and Domenico function as doubles not because they resemble one another psychologically, but because they occupy analogous temporal positions. Each is stranded between belief and action, past and future. The mirror sequences literalize this relation, but the deeper doubling occurs at the level of time: Domenico externalizes Andrei's inner crisis, just as Andrei interiorizes Domenico's mission.

Dreams Without Markers

One of the most radical aspects of *Nostalghia* is Tarkovsky's refusal to mark dreams as dreams. Conventional cinema signals memory through visual codes—fades, dissolves, altered color palettes. Tarkovsky instead relies on imperceptible changes in light, sound, and rhythm. The result is not confusion but suspension. The viewer is forced to remain within the image rather than stepping outside it to decode meaning. The hotel-room sequence exemplifies this strategy. The emergence of the dog—simultaneously a memory and a physical presence—prevents the scene from stabilizing as either dream or reality. The image becomes crystalline: the past is not recalled; it is present.

Water, Ruins, and the Material Past

Water functions throughout *Nostalghia* as a temporal medium. Rain falls indiscriminately across landscapes; pools collect debris and relics alike. Water does not cleanse; it preserves. It saturates the environment with traces of what has been.

Deleuze describes certain elements as "seeds" that generate crystalline environments. In *Nostalghia*, water is such a seed. It belongs to the present as weather, to the past as memory, and to the sacred as residue. Because water appears everywhere, it erodes spatial and temporal distinction. Italy begins to resemble Russia; ruins become homes.

Ruins themselves are not symbols of decay but sites of coexistence. They hold multiple temporal layers at once: what was, what remains, and what can no longer be restored. Tarkovsky does not romanticize ruins; he dwells within them.

Chronosigns: Peaks and Sheets of Time

Deleuze's chronosigns further clarify Tarkovsky's temporal construction. "Peaks of the present" describe moments in which multiple temporal dimensions coexist within a single event. "Sheets of the past" describe the past as a virtual archive preserved in its entirety. Andrei inhabits both structures simultaneously. His encounters with Eugenia, his memories of Russia, and his engagement with Domenico are not sequential phases but concurrent temporal pressures. The film does not ask which time is "real"; it shows that none can be isolated. The candle-crossing scene condenses this logic. The drained pool exposes the past as ruin, yet the act performed within it restores the past as obligation. The present becomes a narrow bridge across an abyss of time.

Derrida's Cinders and the Persistence of the Past

Jacques Derrida's notion of "cinders" provides a powerful metaphor for Tarkovsky's treatment of memory. Cinders are what remain after fire: fragile, dispersed, yet irreducible. They are not origins but residues. In Nostalghia, the past exists as cinders scattered across the landscape—waterlogged ruins, abandoned objects, half-erased rituals. These remnants do not explain the present; they haunt it. Like Derrida's trace, they are neither fully present nor absent. Importantly, cinders resist recovery. One cannot rebuild the fire from ashes. Similarly, Andrei cannot return to Russia, nor can he reconstruct a coherent past. Nostalgia thus becomes exposure to irreversibility rather than desire for restoration.

Nietzsche and Eternal Recurrence

Nietzsche's doctrine of eternal recurrence deepens this temporal logic. Eternal recurrence does not mean repetition of identical events; it affirms the repetition of becoming itself. What returns is not content but form. In *Nostalghia*, repetition takes the form of endurance. Andrei's candle-crossing echoes Domenico's sacrifice, but it does not redeem it. What recurs is the demand to act without guarantee. Identity is not recovered through return; it is undone. Nietzsche's emphasis on intensity rather than continuity resonates strongly here. The candle-crossing is significant not because it succeeds, but because it is endured. Meaning arises not from outcome but from commitment.

Spectatorship and Ethical Demand

One of the most important consequences of Tarkovsky's temporal construction is its effect on the spectator. The viewer is denied interpretive mastery. There is no privileged temporal vantage point from which the film can be organized. Instead, the spectator must endure the film's duration much as Andrei endures his task. This produces an ethical dimension to spectatorship. The viewer is asked not to understand but to remain attentive—to wait, to hesitate, to persist.

Tarkovsky thus transforms cinema into an ethical encounter. To watch *Nostalghia* is to submit to time rather than consume narrative.

Conclusion: Endurance, Sacrifice, and a Time That Remains

Nostalghia is not a film about returning home. It is a film about what remains when return is no longer possible. Tarkovsky replaces nostalgia as longing with nostalgia as exposure—to time, to loss, to obligation. The past persists not as a recoverable origin but as a material remainder scattered across landscapes, rituals, and bodies. The present does not reconcile these fragments; it fractures under their weight. Through crystalline images and chronosigns, Tarkovsky constructs a cinema in which time no longer serves narrative or identity. Instead, time becomes a burden that must be carried—slowly, attentively, without guarantee. The candle-crossing epitomizes this condition. It is an action stripped of symbolic payoff, performed not to achieve meaning but to remain faithful to a demand whose origin cannot be secured.

Read through Derrida's cinders, the past in *Nostalghia* appears as residue rather than foundation—irreducible, fragile, and inescapable. Read through Nietzsche's eternal recurrence, repetition emerges not as restoration but as intensification, affirming becoming without promising reconciliation. What returns is not the self, nor the homeland, nor even belief, but the necessity of endurance itself. In compelling the spectator to inhabit this temporal uncertainty, Tarkovsky transforms cinema into an ethical experience. To watch *Nostalghia* is not to decode a meaning but to submit to time's persistence—to wait, to hesitate, to continue without resolution. In this sense, *Nostalghia* stands as one of modern cinema's most uncompromising meditations on time: a film that does not console but remains.

Works Cited

Augustine. *Confessions*. Translated by R. S. Pine-Coffin, New American Library, 1963.

Braudy, Leo, and Marshall Cohen, editors. *Film Theory and Criticism: Introductory Readings*. 5th ed., Oxford UP, 1999.

Deleuze, Gilles. *Cinema 2: The Time-Image*. Translated by Hugh Tomlinson and Robert Galeta, University of Minnesota Press, 1989.

Deleuze, Gilles, and Félix Guattari. *Anti-Oedipus: Capitalism and Schizophrenia*. Translated by Robert Hurley, Mark Seem, and Helen R. Lane, University of Minnesota Press, 1983.

Derrida, Jacques. *Cinders*. Translated and edited by Ned Lukacher, University of Nebraska Press, 1991.

Goulding, Daniel J., editor. *Five Filmmakers: Tarkovsky, Forman, Polanski, Szabó, Makavejev*. Indiana UP, 1994.

Johnson, Vida T., and Graham Petrie. *The Films of Andrei Tarkovsky: A Visual Fugue*. Indiana UP, 1994.

Nietzsche, Friedrich. *The Will to Power.* Translated by Walter Kaufmann and R. J. Hollingdale, Vintage, 1968.

Ricoeur, Paul. *Time and Narrative*. Translated by Kathleen McLaughlin and David Pellauer, 3 vols., University of Chicago Press, 1984–1986.

Rodowick, D. N. *Gilles Deleuze's Time Machine*. Duke UP, 1997.

Tarkovsky, Andrei. *Sculpting in Time: Reflections on the Cinema.* Translated by Kitty Hunter-Blair, Alfred A. Knopf, 1987.

CHAPTER THREE

Film, Philosophy, and Literature: Fractious Marriages and Multiplicitous Lineages

Introduction: Toward a Schematic of Intertwined Practices

The entanglement of philosophy, film, and literature has often been described in terms of kinship, marriage, or familial tension. Such metaphors suggest a certain inevitability—an ontological or genealogical proximity—yet they also foreground deep structural difficulties that arise when distinct modes of thought attempt to share conceptual or aesthetic territory.

Jason Wesley Alvis, reviewing *Terrence Malick: Film and Philosophy* (a volume I co-edited), turns to a metaphor furnished by Malick himself. Jack's opening voice-over in *The Tree of Life*—"Mother. Father. Always you wrestle inside me. Always you will."—becomes emblematic of the constitutive tension between film and philosophy. Robert Sinnerbrink, in *New Philosophies of Film: Thinking Images*, adopts similar marital language, noting that the union of film and philosophy is "sometimes felicitous, sometimes fractious," while raising a provocative question: which partner, within this marriage, functions as mother or father? These metaphors are not merely ornamental; they carry analytical weight, gesturing toward hierarchical dynamics, generative tensions, and the ambivalent labor of inheritance.

Stanley Cavell's philosophical film criticism and Jean-Luc Godard's philosophically saturated filmmaking represent two radically different models of this marriage. Cavell seeks a form of interlocution between film and philosophy grounded in mutual acknowledgment and moral seriousness; Godard collapses disciplinary distinctions altogether in a promiscuous montage aesthetic. Situated between them, Terrence Malick offers a cinematic meditation on ontology—mediated through literature, theology, and philosophy—that complicates any simple account of disciplinary marriage.

This paper traces these three positions, not to reconcile them, but to sketch a conceptual schema of how philosophy, literature, and cinema coexist: kinships both necessary and troubled; marriages both productive and unstable.

Cavell and the Logic of Necessary Marriages

Cavell's work repeatedly positions the marriage of philosophy and film (and likewise philosophy and literature) as both indispensable and fraught. In The World Viewed, Cavell laments how difficult it is for cinema to present believable families. This difficulty is not accidental; it stems from cinema's structural commitment to the photographic—a medium Cavell identifies as both "automatic" and "without intention." Cinema's very ontology makes the stable presentation of intimacy precarious.

Terrence Malick's *The Tree of Life* provides a paradigmatic case. Its family structure is underwritten by the mother's distinction between "the way of nature" and "the way of grace." The film's metaphysical dyad—nature as self-assertive, grace as self-effacing—manifests in the characters' bodily comportments, gestures, and fragmented memories. "Most commentators," as the essay notes, align the mother with grace ("accepts being slighted… accepts insults and injuries") and the father with nature (seeking self-pleasure, eliciting fear).

This marriage of grace and nature yields three sons, the eldest of whom addresses God implicitly in the film's opening: "Brother. Mother. It was they who led me to your door." The "your" invokes not an abstract deity but God the Father in the Book of Job, announced through the film's epigraph from Job 38:4,7.

Malick thus uses familial language to open a theological and philosophical inquiry. The marriage in the film mirrors a marriage of disciplines: philosophy–theology, film–literature, grace–nature. Cavell's insight—that cinema struggles to render believable families—here becomes a diagnostic tool: Malick's family is unbelievable because it is also allegorical, a staging of irresolvable metaphysical conflict.

Malick, Job, and the Ontological Question

Malick's invocation of Job is not a mere literary flourish. Job's text stages an ancient father–son conflict in which God interrogates Job with questions designed to expose human finitude: "Where were you when I laid the foundations of the earth?" The dialogue exemplifies what Heidegger later formulates as the ontological difference between Being and beings. Heidegger insists that questions concerning Being are unusual. Heidegger:

“To philosophize is to inquire into the extraordinary. But because this question turns back on itself, not only is what is being asked extraordinary, but the act of asking itself is also. In other words, this questioning does not lie along our path for us to stumble upon unexpectedly…nor is it part of everyday life."

The power of such questioning lies in our act of asking (in a sense, Dasein itself is this questioning). They recoil on themselves, demand suspension of everydayness, and resist resolution. Being is not a being; it is a “no-thing,” accessible only through a kind of phenomenological restraint. What Malick omits in his use of the biblical text are the verses just before his chosen passage, which introduce an aggressive exchange between God and Job. Here, God's profound questions come in response to Job's claim of his right to demand answers from God—being to Being. In response, God issues a challenge: "Who is this that darkens counsel by words without knowledge? Gird up your loins like a man; I will question you, and you will declare to me." A flood of questions follows this statement, and Job initially responds by admitting his speechlessness. Yet God repeats His challenge, saying again, "Gird up your loins like a man; I will question you, and you will declare to me," followed by more probing questions.

The exchange highlights a critical shift: it's one thing to question Being, but what happens when Being questions us? Job's questions to God as his son center on justice, yet God demands that Job answer questions about his power as Job's creator-Father. Refusing to engage on these terms, Job ultimately remains silent, resigning himself and, in a sense, giving up. Malick's decision to depart from the verses in which God rebukes Job and instead use the cosmic interrogatives shifts the register of the film: it foregrounds ontology rather than morality, being rather than justice. The film's "cosmic montage"—a long sequence with minimal dialogue—renders God's answer not in speech but in images: the formation of galaxies, oceans, cells, creatures. The montage does not simply illustrate cosmogenesis; it enacts what Heidegger calls worlding—the emergence of a meaningful world. One moment crystallizes this gesture: a dinosaur lifts its foot above a dying companion. The foot hovers between violence and care. It gently lowers rather than crushes. This proto-ethical ambiguity mirrors Mr. O'Brien's oscillation between harshness and tenderness with his sons. The sequence raises questions central to the film and to Job: Is grace immanent within nature? Is nature capable of grace? Or is the distinction itself a human imposition?

Malick therefore stages his film within the unhappy marriage of philosophy and theology—an onto-theological configuration Heidegger famously criticizes but which Malick reanimates cinematically.

Beyond Philosophy and Theology: Fidelity, Adaptation, and Film–Literary Relations

If the marriage of philosophy and theology is strained to the breaking point, what of the marriage between philosophy and film, or between film and literature? Debates on fidelity in film adaptation often assume a hierarchical relationship, positioning literature as original and film as derivative. Yet fidelity, as theorists of translation remind us, is not equivalence but transformation, translative. Film translates literature into another semiotic system—kinetic, visual, auditory, affective.

This translational model provides a framework for turning to Godard, whose relationship to literature and philosophy is radically different from Cavell's. Where Cavell seeks acknowledgment, responsibility, and moral seriousness, Godard approaches texts as raw material for a new cinematic language. His practice exemplifies not fidelity but appropriation, not translation but transposition.

Godard's Polygamy: Literature, Philosophy, and Cinema

Jean-Luc Godard relates to literature, philosophy, and cinema in a manner that refuses simple hierarchy. He treats all three as available partners—as simultaneous spouses in a plural marriage. His antagonism toward screenwriting ("I hate writing") coexists with a voracious citational impulse. Texts function as fragments, idioms, voices that "are there," waiting to be inserted into new cinematic constellations.

By his own account, Godard's discovery of cinema did not come from seeing a great film but from reading André Gide's prose poem Fruits of the Earth, a literary work. He might have pursued a literary career, but, as he told Marguerite Duras, "I hate writing. Not writing in itself, but the moment in which it comes—all that time." He continued, "I don't write texts since they exist." Yet his years as a film critic at *Cahiers du Cinéma* cultivated a subjective, polemical voice—one capable of bridging argument and confession, agreement and provocation. Cavell describes art as requiring the ability to speak from one's subjectivity while claiming universality. But cinema appealed to Godard because it allowed for a more impersonal form of expression, a certain automatism. Writing felt too naked, too intimate, while at the same time, too chaste. Film offered Godard, as Cavell notes, a sterile medium whose promiscuity—the ability to combine with music, text, image, typography"—enabled new modes of aesthetic and philosophical engagement.

Citational Montage: Godard's Subjectile Aesthetic

Godard's cinematic language is fundamentally citational. He thus brings philosophy and literature into dialogue through cinema, using film as a means of exploration without the constraints of authorship that writing imposes. Philosophy, literature, and cinema coalesce into a three-way conversation through spoken dialogue, much like Derrida's philosophical literary explorations. Like Derrida, Godard takes full advantage of the French language's natural inclination for wordplay, using puns, double meanings, and ambiguities, often without attribution. His films operate as subjectiles—a term borrowed from Artaud—

meaning surfaces that support layered inscriptions, erasures, and overwritings.

For example, in *Breathless*—one of only two Godard films praised by Cavell, the other being Alphaville—Michel and Patricia go to the movies to hide out and watch the American Western Westbound. In a brief scene, we see a close-up of the two lovers kissing, with dialogue from Westbound playing in the background. The dialogue is barely audible, not only to us but presumably to the characters as diegetic sound. However, the dialogue we hear is not from the Westbound soundtrack. Instead, the soundtrack is overwritten by snippets from two combined poems, one by Apollinaire and the other by Aragon, modified, blended, and spoken not by the characters, but by Godard and Jean Seberg as themselves. Godard changes the original poems freely, disregarding fidelity to the poetic texts and the Westbound dialogue. This form destabilizes the diegesis. The sound does not "match" the image; instead, it forms a counterpoint, a refusal of conventional cinematic suturing. The moment anticipates practices of sampling, remixing, and montage that would define late-20th-century media art.

Godard frequently films characters reading aloud from literature, philosophy, sociology, or art history—activities rarely considered cinematic. "Readings are just fantastic!" he claimed. "The most fantastic thing you could film is people reading." The act of reading becomes an event, a performance, a source of cinematic energy.

Stuart Kendall's analysis in Phrases: Six Films demonstrates the extent of Godard's citational method: the screenplay for Nouvelle Vague is assembled almost entirely from texts collected by Hervé Duhmal—Chandler, Hemingway, Faulkner, Dostoevsky, Gide, Bataille, Novarina, and Char. Jonathan Dronesfield notes that Godard treats the book "as if it were a persona… the impersonal 'it speaks'." Text and image do not compete in Godard; they interpenetrate, forming new discursive circuits.

Cavell's Critique: Depersonalization and the Loss of Subjectivity

Cavell remains deeply skeptical of Godard's method. He argues that Godard's citational practice depersonalizes characters, transforming them into conduits for "it speaks." They possess no individuating biography, no temporality, no recognizable subjectivity. They exist as idiomatic vessels for slogans, fragments, or philosophical lines.

For Cavell, the world already dehumanizes subjects; to multiply slogans is to exacerbate the crisis. Art must justify its moral and philosophical commitments: "What entitles him to our attention is precisely his responsibility to this condition." Godard, Cavell believes, refuses this responsibility, basking in the aesthetic of depersonalization.

Two examples clarify the critique:

1. Godard's camera tests of women, which Cavell reads as reducing feminine

subjects to surfaces—commodities echoing advertising, pornography, and prostitution.

2. The philosophical dialogue in My Life to Live between Nana and Brice Parain, which Cavell finds seductive but empty, undermining the rigor and vulnerability philosophy demands.

Cavell's complaint is not prudishness but ethics: philosophy, when invoked, should become a "nobler seduction"—one that teaches love as the "power to accept intimacy without taking it personally." Godard flirts with philosophy but never consummates the union responsibly.

Conclusion: Community, Families, and Plural Marriages of the Arts

Philosophy, modern literature, and modernist cinema share a concern with the conditions of their own possibility. As Cavell writes, "when three stand on the same ground, there is community." One might just as well say family—or plural marriage. Yet families fracture; marriages strain; communities falter. The shared ground is not a foundation but a contested terrain requiring constant negotiation.

If one of these partners—philosophy, film, literature—calls its own existence into question and simultaneously reaffirms it, its responsibility becomes acute. Cavell's closing insight sharpens the stakes: responsibility lies not merely in forging connections between mediums, but in how one inhabits the shared ground such connections create.

Malick, Cavell, and Godard illuminate three different modes of marital responsibility:

- Cavell seeks acknowledgment, intimacy, moral seriousness.
- Malick turns to theological and ontological inheritance, staging cosmic questions through cinematic worlding.

- Godard refuses monogamy altogether, embracing promiscuous textuality.

The resulting marriages—felicitous, fractious, plural—testify not only to the capacity of film, philosophy, and literature to cohabit the same conceptual space, but to the ethical demands placed on any artist who attempts to bring them together.

www.ingramcontent.com/pod-product-compliance
Lightning Source LLC
LaVergne TN
LVHW050610100826
845148LV00015B/3212

* 9 7 9 8 9 0 2 4 3 1 3 9 8 *